MW01615736

Brilliant Ideas

I Had While

Taking A Dump

Published by Upgraded Books

Tak|ing A Dump
[tayk-ing uh dump] *Verb, universal*

The ultimate act of relief, both physically and emotionally. A moment of pure clarity, where life's stresses are flushed away.

It's a time for reflection, solving puzzles, deep thought, and checking your phone for funny memes, messages, and social media.

The dump is an underrated yet essential ritual, providing not just release but also unexpected moments of inspiration.

Synonyms: *Bombs away, these farts aren't funny anymore, I need to take this call, business meeting.*

Toilet Inspired Genius

Fun Fact

The Ancient Romans were ahead of their time with their sophisticated public toilets, aqueducts, and sewer systems.

They had "toilet clubs" where members paid dues to keep public restrooms clean and functional.

Toilet Inspired Genius

Question of the Day

Assuming an unlimited budget, what invention would you create that would dramatically upgrade the toilet experience?

Toilet Inspired Genius

Help The Poo Get
To The Toilet!

Toilet Inspired Genius

Solution

Toilet Inspired Genius

Fun Fact

Contrary to what many believe, silent farts aren't necessarily smellier than noisy ones.

The stink factor depends on what you've eaten and your body's digestion, not the noise level or volume of your fart.

Toilet Inspired Genius

Question of the Day

What song would you choose to play automatically each time you enter the bathroom?

Toilet Inspired Genius

Flush Out The Words!

H	G	A	S	T	I	N	K	E	R	C	T
J	D	Z	P	B	U	A	E	H	H	I	P
Z	J	E	Q	U	P	G	I	V	G	H	X
U	Y	T	U	M	M	C	G	Q	H	K	P
H	C	B	U	C	W	R	G	F	Z	V	O
P	Z	D	N	R	E	A	Y	T	G	U	O
X	M	A	O	V	D	P	E	O	B	L	P
F	G	O	R	I	G	P	L	O	P	X	L
A	F	P	L	J	I	E	T	T	X	K	B
M	U	O	F	E	E	R	X	W	J	S	T
T	S	O	H	T	A	X	C	W	X	P	H
X	R	X	M	F	R	K	Q	X	K	R	W

GAS	POO	LOG
BUM	FART	TURD
POOP	DUMP	PLOP
LEAK	TOOT	DEUCE
WEDGIE	STINKER	CRAPPER

Toilet Inspired Genius

The Solution Flushed Out

H	G	A	S	T	I	N	K	E	R	C	T
J	D	Z	P	B	U	A	E	H	H	I	P
Z	J	E	Q	U	P	G	I	V	G	H	X
U	Y	T	U	M	M	C	G	Q	H	K	P
H	C	B	U	C	W	R	G	F	Z	V	O
P	Z	D	N	R	E	A	Y	T	G	U	O
X	M	A	O	V	D	P	E	O	B	L	P
F	G	O	R	I	G	P	L	O	P	X	L
A	F	P	L	J	I	E	T	T	X	K	B
M	U	O	F	E	E	R	X	W	J	S	T
T	S	O	H	T	A	X	C	W	X	P	H
X	R	X	M	F	R	K	Q	X	K	R	W

GAS	POO	LOG
BUM	FART	TURD
POOP	DUMP	PLOP
LEAK	TOOT	DEUCE
WEDGIE	STINKER	CRAPPER

Toilet Inspired Genius

Fun Fact

The largest poop in the planet belongs to a proud Viking in the 9th century at just under 8 inches in length.

It was discovered by an archaelogist in 1972 in a semi-fossilized form in England.

Toilet Inspired Genius

Question of the Day

If you could choose which celebrity was present in the public bathroom you were in, who would it be and why?

Toilet Inspired Genius

Break The Bathroom Code!

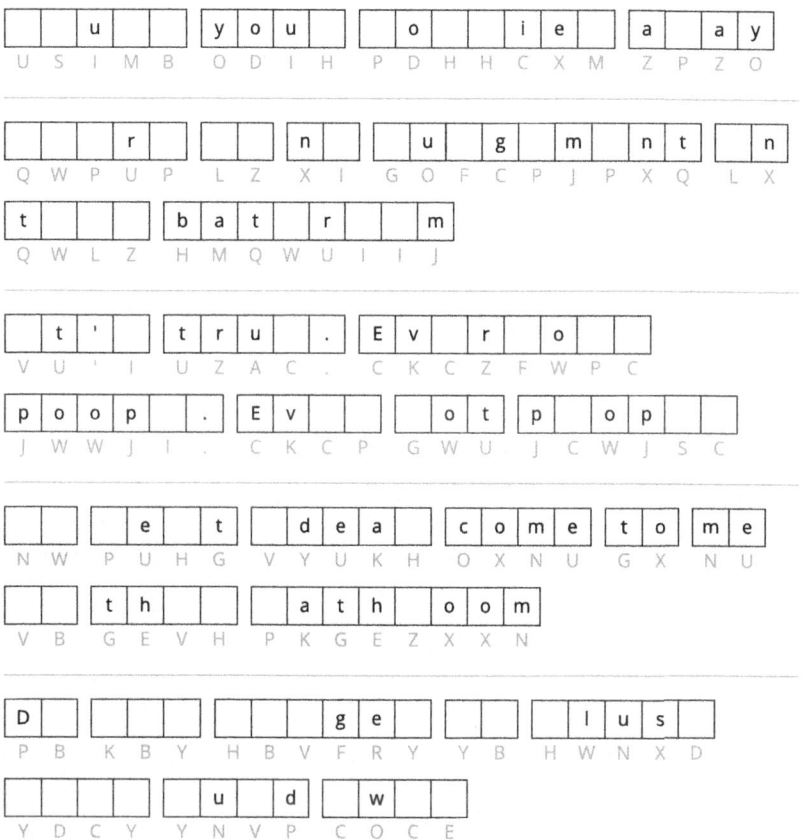

Toilet Inspired Genius

Unclogged Answers

Flush your worries away

There is no judgement in this bathroom

It's true. Everyone poops. Even hot people

My best ideas come to me in this bathroom

Do not forget to flush that turd away

Toilet Inspired Genius

Fun Fact

Whale poop is a fertilizer for the sea.

In addition to whale poo being massive, it is also essential for the ocean's ecosystem.

It's rich in iron and nitrogen, which helps stimulate phytoplankton growth — tiny organisms that are the base of the marine food chain.

Toilet Inspired Genius

Question of the Day

If toilets could talk, what would yours say?

Toilet Inspired Genius

Crossword for the Crapper

Across:
1. A fixture designed for washing after using the toilet which is especially popular in Europe
4. Tiny ocean organisms
5. Poop used to fertilize crops
8. A cosmetic item typically used while getting ready in the bathroom
9. This prevents dryness

Down:
2. The material that toilets are made of
3. Someone very concerned about hygiene
6. The scientific term for farting
7. The formal term for poop
10. When the toilet is clogged, you need this

Toilet Inspired Genius

Crapper Solutions

Across:
1. A fixture designed for washing after using the toilet which is especially popular in Europe
4. Tiny ocean organisms
5. Poop used to fertilize crops
8. A cosmetic item typically used while getting ready in the bathroom
9. This prevents dryness

Down:
2. The material that toilets are made of
3. Someone very concerned about hygiene
6. The scientific term for farting
7. The formal term for poop
10. When the toilet is clogged, you need this

Crossword answers (grid):

2 Down: PORCELAINS
3 Down: GERMOPHOB
1 Across: BIDET
7 Down: EXCREMENT
6 Down: FLATULENCE
4 Across: PLANKTON
8 Across: CONCEALER
10 Down: PLUGE
5 Across: MANURE
9 Across: MOISTURIZE

Toilet Inspired Genius

Fun Fact

When wombats take a dump, they produce cube-shaped poops.

One theory for why this could be is that it prevents the poo from rolling away and making it easier to mark their territory.

Toilet Inspired Genius

Question of the Day

What's the weirdest bathroom moment you've ever experienced?

Toilet Inspired Genius

Prevent Poo-Mageddon!

Help the poo get to the sewage to prevent a catastrophe

Toilet Inspired Genius

Poo-Route

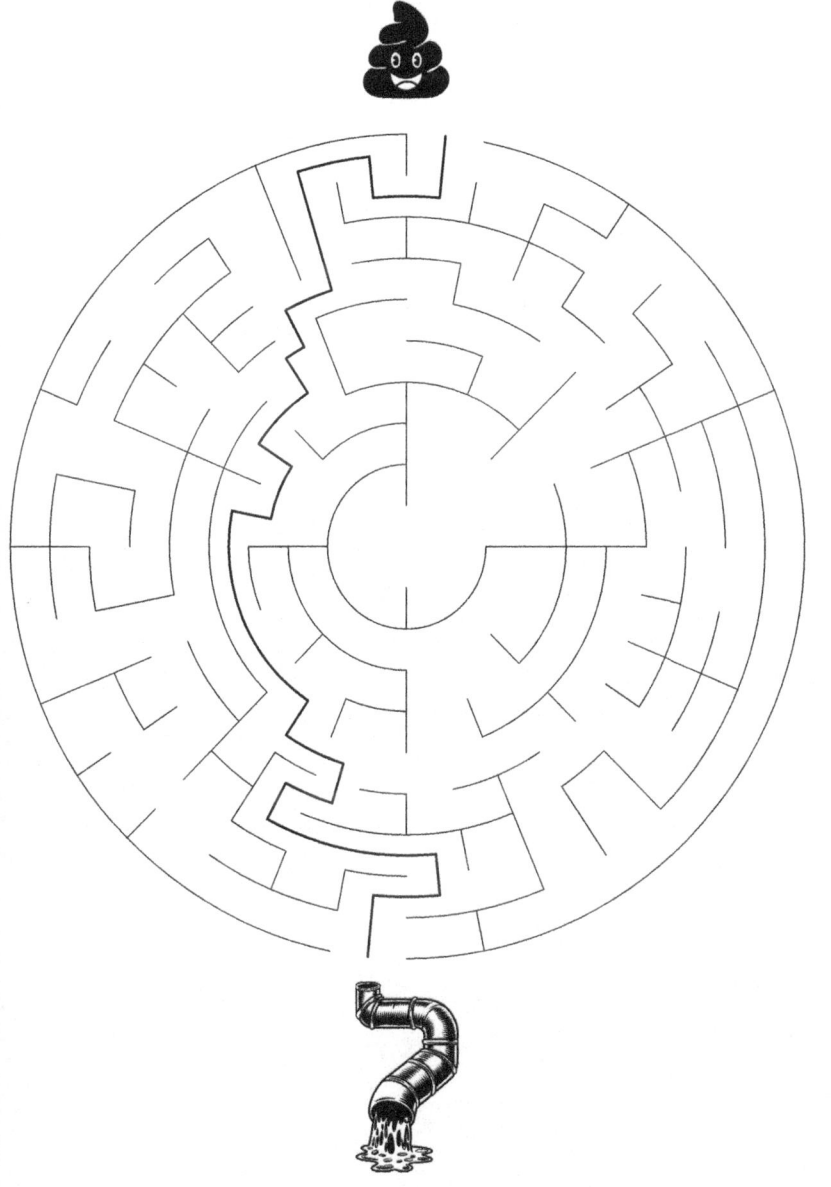

Toilet Inspired Genius

Fun Fact

Bird poop, also known as guano, is rich in nitrogen, phosphorus, and potassium.

It was used historically used to make gunpowder and explosives as well as agricultural fertilizer.

In the 19th century, entire industries were built around mining guano from remote islands.

Toilet Inspired Genius

Question of the Day

What's the weirdest bathroom moment you've ever experienced?

Toilet Inspired Genius

Loo-Doku Puzzle

	5	8				7		
			5		4			8
	7					1		
7	6							
		1				3	8	
8				6	3			
			8	5				
3					7		1	
				3		5	2	

Toilet Inspired Genius

Toilet Triumph

9	5	8	2	1	6	7	3	4
1	3	2	5	7	4	6	9	8
4	7	6	3	9	8	1	5	2
7	6	3	9	8	5	2	4	1
5	9	1	7	4	2	3	8	6
8	2	4	1	6	3	9	7	5
2	1	7	8	5	9	4	6	3
3	4	5	6	2	7	8	1	9
6	8	9	4	3	1	5	2	7

Toilet Inspired Genius

Fun Fact

When shit hits the fan is a popular English expression used when something's about to suddenly become chaotic.

Spanish: To have a fart — To be drunk

German: This shit is steaming — Situation is about to get out of control

Portuguese: To let out a fart — Some that nervously blurts shit out

Polish: I have it in my ass — I don't give a shit

Toilet Inspired Genius

Question of the Day

What was the most embarrassing fart experience you've had?

Toilet Inspired Genius

Fart The Words Out!

```
Z  H  L  L  I  V  I  M  X  S  T  I  Q  Z  J  O  H  M
Z  R  E  G  U  R  G  I  T  A  T  I  O  N  C  E  G  P
L  M  X  A  U  P  M  E  L  R  H  B  O  D  Y  N  A  X
D  I  A  R  R  H  E  A  B  U  P  I  M  T  I  E  G  O
R  Y  F  L  B  T  X  S  W  I  T  O  Z  P  I  S  A  Q
T  J  W  B  L  B  B  H  E  A  J  L  R  G  N  R  R  C
P  R  U  M  O  N  B  U  P  N  U  U  P  W  W  U  I  D
S  U  S  S  A  A  C  I  R  Y  B  X  A  H  E  L  F  L
T  M  B  B  T  U  T  X  N  N  Q  S  D  H  L  U  A  Q
T  B  C  A  I  S  N  V  R  D  L  C  J  E  O  U  R  F
Q  L  M  C  N  E  C  V  O  M  I  T  I  N  G  W  T  L
E  I  Q  O  G  A  L  R  S  P  X  G  I  V  M  Y  I  V
A  N  C  I  G  G  F  L  A  T  U  L  E  N  C  E  N  W
D  G  B  E  A  A  J  H  M  M  B  B  W  S  R  Q  G  K
M  X  M  B  M  S  I  W  E  D  P  R  E  C  T  A  L  I
D  Y  V  V  Q  M  Q  N  T  E  S  W  O  X  I  B  X
F  T  C  M  W  L  N  P  B  W  Q  L  N  E  K  S  O  Y
J  A  I  T  A  R  F  T  J  X  U  C  U  R  O  U  O  N
```

GAS	NAUSEA	CRAMPS
RECTAL	FARTING	BURPING
DIARRHEA	BLOATING	RUMBLING
VOMITING	HEARTBURN	FLATULENCE
INDIGESTION	CONSTIPATION	REGURGITATION

Toilet Inspired Genius

Windy Solutions

Z	H	L	L	I	V	I	M	X	S	T	I	Q	Z	J	O	H	M
Z	R	E	G	U	R	G	I	T	A	T	I	O	N	C	E	G	P
L	M	X	A	U	P	M	E	L	R	H	B	O	D	Y	N	A	X
D	I	A	R	R	H	E	A	B	U	P	I	M	T	I	E	G	O
R	Y	F	L	B	T	X	S	W	I	T	O	Z	P	I	S	A	Q
T	J	W	B	L	B	B	H	E	A	J	L	R	G	N	R	R	C
P	R	U	M	O	N	B	U	P	N	U	U	P	W	W	U	I	D
S	U	S	S	A	A	C	I	R	Y	B	X	A	H	E	L	F	L
T	M	B	B	T	U	T	X	N	N	Q	S	D	H	L	U	A	Q
T	B	C	A	I	S	N	V	R	D	L	C	J	E	O	U	R	F
Q	L	M	C	N	E	C	V	O	M	I	T	I	N	G	W	T	L
E	I	Q	O	G	A	L	R	S	P	X	G	I	V	M	Y	I	V
A	N	C	I	G	G	F	L	A	T	U	L	E	N	C	E	N	W
D	G	B	E	A	A	J	H	M	M	B	B	W	S	R	Q	G	K
M	X	M	B	M	S	I	W	E	D	P	R	E	C	T	A	L	I
D	Y	V	V	Q	M	Q	N	T	E	S	W	O	X	I	B	X
F	T	C	M	W	L	N	P	B	W	Q	L	N	E	K	S	O	Y
J	A	I	T	A	R	F	T	J	X	U	C	U	R	O	U	O	N

GAS	NAUSEA	CRAMPS
RECTAL	FARTING	BURPING
DIARRHEA	BLOATING	RUMBLING
VOMITING	HEARTBURN	FLATULENCE
INDIGESTION	CONSTIPATION	REGURGITATION

Toilet Inspired Genius

Porcelain Poet

Write a funny 4-line poem inspired by your bathroom experience.

Hint: Think about the sounds (plop or farting), the setting (toilet seat or toilet paper), the emotion (bored or relief).

Example:
"Sitting here, I start to think,
Will I make this toilet sink?"

Toilet Inspired Genius

Fun Fact

Sloths only shit about once a week.

When they do so, it's a real event. A sloth's lifestyle is mainly about staying hidden and conserving energy. It can take a sloth an entire month to digest a single leaf, leaving them with little room to burn energy unnecessarily.

To relieve themselves, they come all the way down from their treetops to take their dump on ground level leaving them exposed to predators.

Toilet Inspired Genius

Toilet Paper Origami

Objective:

Create your own piece of toilet paper art while sitting on the throne.

How To Play:

Create shapes using toilet paper like a heart or a diamond. Feel free to use YouTube for any guidance (search "toilet paper origami")

Toilet Inspired Genius

Help The Poo Get Through The Digestive Tract!

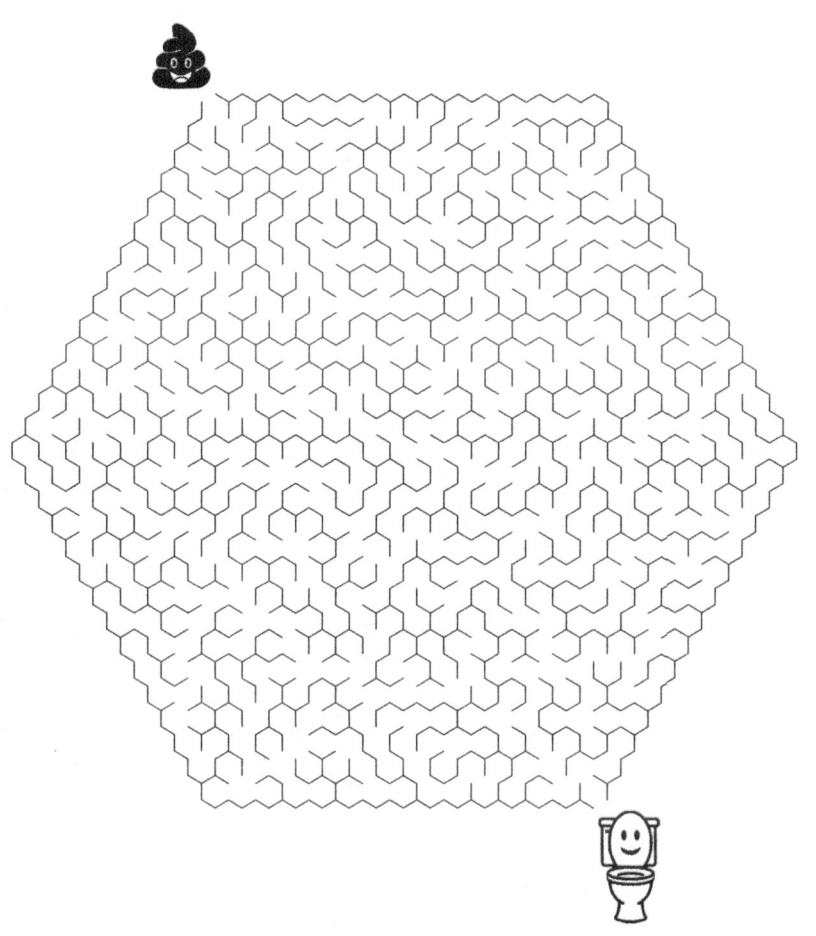

Toilet Inspired Genius

Toilet Inspired Genius

Fun Fact

The smell of poop comes mainly from bacteria breaking down food in the digestive system.

That lovely "natural fragrance" you smell is gases that get released including methane and sulfur.

Toilet Inspired Genius

Ways To Excuse Yourself

Time to punish the porcelain

I need to have a chat with my fart's manager

I'm off to unleash the dogs of war

I've got a code brown situation going on here

I'm about to birth a kraken

Gotta unload the trailer

I'm crowning

Toilet Inspired Genius

Porcelain Bucket List

Create a list of things that you'd like to do while sitting on the toilet.

Some examples include reading a specific book, generate a list of brilliant ideas for vacation, making money, saving the planet, a 30 day challenge of making the bathroom a device-free zone, and so on.

Toilet Inspired Genius

Fun Fact

The brown color of poop is thanks to stercobilin, a pigment that's formed from the breakdown of red blood cells and bile which helps in digesting fats.

The ideal stool color is a yummy chocolatey brown.

Healthy poo will generally sink to the bottom of the toilet bowl.

Toilet Inspired Genius

Toilet Laws

Lay down your own set of bathroom rules that friends, family and visitors must adhere to.

For example, *no phones allowed with the exception of playing relaxing music, no selfies, don't look at the crack between the doors, toilet seat must always be down, and so on.*

Then get creative with the punishment that they will face if the rules are broken.

For example, *must clean the bathroom mirror for the entire week or write a sincere and formal apology letter.*

Toilet Inspired Genius

Toilet Superstitions

Nigeria: *It is believed that spitting directly into a toilet bowl will lead to a sore throat.*

China: *The toilet door should be closed at night because it's believed that evil spirits gather in the bathroom.*

Japan: *Keeping a clean bathroom is said to bring good luck and prosperity.*

Malaysia: *Not washing period pads before throwing them out is said to attract ghosts.*

Philippines: *Bathing on Good Friday after 3 pm is believed to bring bad luck*

Toilet Inspired Genius

Thank you for choosing this book!

I hope you enjoyed this book :)

I would be incredibly grateful if you could take just 30 seconds to leave me a review! Reviews are crucial for an author's livelihood and surprisingly difficult to come by.

The more reviews my books receive, the more I can continue pursuing my love for creating books. If you have any thoughts about this book, please leave a review and let me know.

- Sam

Made in the USA
Coppell, TX
18 December 2024